# Breaking Through to Effective Teaching

*A Walk-Through Protocol Linking Student Learning and Professional Practice*

Patricia Martinez-Miller
Laureen Cervone

*UCLA School Management Program*

With contributions by
Bobby Blatt, Dan Chernow, Lisa DiMartino,
Barbara Linsley, Juan Lopez, and
UCLA SMP Faculty

Rowman & Littlefield Education
Lanham, Maryland • Toronto • Plymouth, UK
2008

Published in the United States of America
by Rowman & Littlefield Education
A Division of Rowman & Littlefield Publishers, Inc.
A wholly owned subsidiary of The Rowman & Littlefield Publishing
Group, Inc.
4501 Forbes Boulevard, Suite 200, Lanham, Maryland 20706
www.rowmaneducation.com

Estover Road
Plymouth PL6 7PY
United Kingdom

British Library Cataloguing in Publication Information Available

**Library of Congress Cataloging-in-Publication Data**

Martinez-Miller, Patricia, 1944–
  Breaking through to effective teaching : a walk-through protocol linking
student learning and professional practice / Patricia Martinez-Miller, Laureen
Cervone.
     p. cm.
  ISBN-13: 978-1-57886-735-6 (hardcover : alk. paper)
  ISBN-13: 978-1-57886-736-3 (pbk. : alk. paper)
  ISBN-10: 1-57886-735-5 (hardcover : alk. paper)
  ISBN-10: 1-57886-736-3 (pbk. : alk. paper)
  1. Effective teaching. 2. Inquiry-based learning. I. Cervone, Laureen, 1957-
II. Title.
  LB1025.3.M3376 2008
  371.102—dc22                                    2007041463

♾™ The paper used in this publication meets the minimum requirements of
American National Standard for Information Sciences—Permanence of Paper
for Printed Library Materials, ANSI/NISO Z39.48-1992.
Manufactured in the United States of America.

# TABLE OF CONTENTS

# Preface

This is a modest, practical book with a powerful, revolutionary purpose. The authors present a clear, concise set of protocols for conducting walk-throughs, linking leadership practice directly to the improvement of instruction in classrooms. This book gets as close to practical guidance in how to do the work as one can without actually being directly coached by experts. In this sense, it is the most powerful text for practitioners available in this critical area of practice.

But this book has significance far beyond its immediate practical usefulness. It can also be read as a powerful, counter-cultural manifesto about the nature of practice in education. I have argued that education is a profession without a practice. That is, educators lack a common language for talking about their practice and a common set of protocols for defining their practice with each other. One could argue that the existence of a common practice, in this sense, is the defining characteristic of a "real" profession. It is the existence of a practice that allows professions to do what professions are supposed to do: develop a common culture that defines the expertise of their members, to exercise control over membership in the profession according to whether individuals have mastered the practice, and to exercise social authority regarding the terms and conditions of their practice. Absent a well-defined body of practice, educators are people to whom things are done, *not* people who exercise significant control over the conditions of their practice. The current systems of accountability in which educators operate under rules and structures that are largely at odds with their capacity to engage in high-level practice, are a case in point for what happens in a profession without a practice.

What the authors of this book have done is to begin the conversation about what it means to have a practice in the profession of education. Their experience developing protocols, structures, and processes for educators to engage in high-level analysis of their practice is critical to the development of a common body of knowledge for a profession of education. The level of detail, the practical focus, the clarity, and logic of this model are exemplary, and they set a standard for future work in the field.

I have, for the past seven years, been engaged in a similar initiative with school superintendents and principals in the northeastern United States. Without consciously collaborating, I discovered through serendipity that I was working on a model that is virtually identical in its main elements to the work of the School Management Program (SMP) at UCLA. Meeting and sharing experiences with the SMP group has been one of the highlights of my recent professional experience. We have together since discovered allies in other parts of the country who are working on similar ideas, and have jointly benefited from their experience.

In the history of professions, this is how major changes occur: Practitioners and researchers with a consuming interest in practice combine forces to develop new institutional arrangements based on new cultural assumptions about the nature of practice. The U.S. medical profession, for example, did not develop as an offshoot of conventional institutions, nor from formal policy declarations. It developed by creating a new set of institutions—the exemplar was the Johns Hopkins University Medical School—based on an entirely new model of medical practice, and an entirely new model of medical education, and then using those institutions to displace the resident culture.

This book begins the process of reconstituting educational practice and bringing education to a new level of understanding of the relationship between professional knowledge, professional practice, and the processes of organization and management of educational institutions.

Richard Elmore, Ed.D.
Gregory R. Anrig Professor of Educational
Leadership Director,
Consortium for Policy Research in Education,
Harvard University

# INTRODUCTION

Since 1992, the UCLA School Management Program (UCLA SMP) has supported public K-12 schools in their efforts to improve student learning and achievement. A nonprofit school reform center of the Graduate School of Education & Information Studies, the **UCLA School Management Program** is committed to the sustainable transformation of public schools into learner-centered organizations where all students achieve at high levels. UCLA SMP is located on the UCLA campus, with a regional office serving the northeastern United States in Trumbull, Connecticut.

Our group of practitioner faculty—teachers, administrators, district office personnel, organizational specialists, and school board members—has facilitated improvement in student learning in hundreds of schools and multiple districts. Professional reflection and understanding of the leadership and beliefs that create a school culture that results in high levels of student learning and achievement is core to UCLA SMP's work.

This book will lead the reader step by step though the philosophy and implementation of the UCLA SMP Walk-Through protocol. Our desire for you, the reader, is that the Walk-Through protocol becomes such a part of your culture that there is no controversy about it, and that teachers are extremely comfortable walking into each other's classrooms. This is a *conversational* process where peers learn together. You will not find any instructional checklists in these pages; this process does not ask the question, "Are we doing it right?" Rather, it leads to collaborative conversation and action based on the question, "Is what we are doing resulting in the student learning we envision?"

Chapter 1 provides an overview of the process and some of the research on which it is based. The chapter helps answer questions about a school's readiness to use Walk-Throughs as an integral part of sustainable improvement in student learning.

Chapter 2 introduces the "Nuts and Bolts" of the UCLA SMP Walk-Through protocol. This chapter is the "user guide" to effective use of this tool as part of a cycle of continuous improvement. Readers will understand what to do before, during, and after the walk. They will be prepared to develop the focus question that drives the classroom visit.

Chapter 3 takes us into the Walk-Through process as a way to connect curriculum, instruction, assessment, and professional development. The chapter focuses on how the process is used to drive and build sustainable change. A clear and concise connection to UCLA SMP's Cycle of Continuous Improvement is explored.

The next three chapters are case studies that illustrate the Walk-Through protocol in action. These case studies are real examples of how and where schools using the protocol have made significant changes in student learning and achievement.

Chapter 4 presents the story of the Six to Six Magnet School in Bridgeport, Connecticut. This school used the Walk-Through protocol to foster and sustain a professional learning community. Chapter 5 recounts the inquiry at Suva Elementary School in Montebello,

California, a state-identified "underperforming" school that used the Walk-Through protocol to achieve significant gains in standardized test scores and to promote student learning and understanding through improved instructional practice. Chapter 6 describes a whole-district reform effort in California's Antelope Valley Union High School District. This improving district chose to use the Walk-Through protocol to facilitate a coherent, systemic dialogue about instructional practices, district practices, and student results across many schools.

This book will serve as a resource for your own questions and learning about how the UCLA School Management Program Walk-Through protocol can help you create and sustain a culture of continuous improvement in your district, school, and classroom. We welcome you to our growing learning community.

Dan Chernow, Ed.D., Executive Director
UCLA School Management Program

# Chapter 1.  Why Walk-Throughs?

"The purpose of the Walk-Through is really to provide an opportunity to have conversations with each other about what is happening in classrooms, so teachers can make change in the classroom. They can see what the current reality is, work together to gather data, and use that information to build on the strengths that are already there."—10th grade teacher, Brockton High School, Brockton, Massachusetts

Understanding what it means to assure a "quality public education" is evolving at an exponential rate. Schools across our nation are struggling to keep up with rising standards, changing technology, and widely diverse student bodies with unique needs. This struggle is played out in an increasingly public forum focused on results. We know that the "factory model" of education is no longer valid in our knowledge-based society. Schools that are successful today have taken different paths, but all function as learning communities that hold some characteristics in common. Walk-Throughs, as part of a teacher-driven cycle of improvement, provide the structure to achieve an effective and sustainable learning community that supports excellent teaching and increasingly high levels of student achievement.

## Building on our own best practice

Nearly twenty years of educational research suggest that effective schools maintain a defined focus on student results. Research links improved student results directly to improved teacher practice. Further, studies identify teacher "learning communities" as the context for professional development most likely to improve instructional practice.

In a 2004 Phi Delta Kappan article entitled *Tipping Point: From Feckless Reform to Substantive Instructional Improvement[1]*, Mike Schmoker pointed out how rare learning communities are in our schools. He wrote, "Though such terms as 'learning communities' and 'lesson study' are heard more than ever, we hardly acknowledge their central importance in actual practice: it is a rare school that has established regular times for teachers to create, test, and refine their lessons and strategies together."

The Walk-Through protocol developed and employed by UCLA's School Management Program is a deceptively simple process that has fostered transformation in schools across the country. Drawing from the research on effective schools, it is built on three core beliefs:

1. All students have the ability to master a rigorous, standards-based curriculum.
2. Classroom teachers want to grow as professionals and constantly improve their craft.
3. The greatest leverage point for transformational growth in student achievement exists

---

[1] Schmoker, M. (February 2004). *Tipping Point: From Feckless Reform to Substantive Instructional Improvement.* In *Phi Delta Kappan.*

in the classroom; in the interaction between the student, the teacher, and the content.

The Walk-Through protocol is a "content-neutral" process. It is designed to help teachers gain a deeper understanding of the results of their current practice—and implement the kind of changes that improve practice to improve results. It is about teachers figuring out what they need, rather than acting on a directive from outside the classroom telling them what they need.

The Walk-Through team begins by choosing an area for their inquiry and crafts a *focus question* about student learning in the classroom. This may be as narrow as a small group of biology teachers wondering about student understanding of the circulatory system, or as broad as a district wondering about the engagement of students across all classes.

Using the focus question as a guide, "walkers" visit classrooms in their own school to collect evidence of what students are

---

Think about your own classroom. Perhaps your school's mission statement mentions students being "engaged" in their learning, or perhaps student engagement is something you have been working on. It is often incorporated in a state's standards for the teaching profession.

Take a moment to reflect:
- How engaged are your students in their own learning?
- How do you know? (What is your evidence?)
- What does engagement look like?
- What difference might it make if your students were more engaged?

---

doing or saying in the classroom. Walkers are challenged to act like a video camera and make their observations factual, without opinion or evaluation. All of the observations are brought together and shared when the team convenes for the debriefing session. Evidence is read and charted for all to see—without mentioning student or teacher names or room numbers.

The team then begins to search for patterns or themes among the evidence and raise questions about what they have seen. At first, answering the questions seems simple. But after visiting classrooms, observing students, talking with colleagues about what you saw and wondering about the instruction-learning connection, it becomes a little murkier.

It is this reflective discussion that leads to naming a specific "better result" and sets the stage for suggesting "next steps"—things that *might* lead to improvement in student understanding.

The Walk-Through protocol does not lead to changes by itself. We have placed the protocol into a cycle of continuous improvement, much like an action research cycle, where teachers are challenged to do something different in their classrooms and then given the opportunity to assess the results on student learning. The cycle of improvement supports hypothesis generation and testing, with real-time data collection bringing you closer to your stated goal for student results.

## Why this is a different approach

School communities develop action plans to assure high student achievement as a matter of course. Professional development figures prominently in these plans, so schools and districts labor to create professional development plans that will make a difference in student learning. Most plans aim to be data driven. They begin with a look at student achievement results; they set improvement goals and initiate professional learning based on specific, research-validated instructional strategies. Teachers commonly learn together and share their experiences as a community. Yet, with the best of intentions, the results of professional development often fail to provide the universally high student achievement that educators envision.

In *Building a New Structure for School Leadership*, Richard Elmore writes, "Standards based reform hits at a critical weakness of the existing institutional structure, namely its inability to account for why certain students master academic content while others do not. When the core of schooling is buried in the individual decisions of classroom teachers and buffered from external scrutiny, outcomes are the consequence of mysterious processes that no one understands at the collective, institutional level. Therefore, we are free to assign causality to whatever our favorite theory suggests: weak family structures, poverty, discrimination, lack of aptitude, television."[2]

---

[2] Elmore, R.F. (2000). *Building a new structure for school leadership.* Washington DC: The Albert Shanker Institute.

In the chapters that follow we introduce a protocol that is organically tied to student results. This protocol uses a teacher-developed focus question to link observed student learning to inquiry about instructional practice. It calls on participants to see and record like video cameras, assuring the collection of data, not opinion. Finally, it fosters conversations across the teaching community—and at its most powerful, across the whole school community—to surface positive patterns and trends and to frame inquiry and action to obtain even greater positive student impact.

## *How the Walk-Through protocol supports success*

Effective learning communities exist where participants trust each other. The Walk-Through protocol facilitates that community by providing processes and structures that ground observations and conversations in inquiry, not judgment. The protocol never asks "who" is effective. Instead, it helps teachers determine "what" is effective for their students. The teacher-generated focus question links student understanding to the instructional practices in which the understanding evolved. Teachers strive to understand how students understand, so future lessons benefit from teacher learning about the efficacy of current lessons. Patterns and trends in student learning that teachers want to see more of are the catalysts for professional development and instructional experimentation. With each successive walk-through, the instructional actions taken result in deeper student understanding and higher achievement.

For many teachers, professional development often feels disconnected from their day-to-day work with students. Formal opportunities to learn together can be perceived as add-ons to their work, rather than as integral to their growth as professionals. The Walk-Through protocol counters this by providing a teacher-driven context for data collection, analysis, new learning and new action. Here, professional development is integrated into teachers' ongoing work. Teachers themselves decide on the results they wish to influence; they identify the practice they will alter to change the results; they determine what they need to know in order to be more effective; and they define how they will know if they are successful.

## *When are schools ready for the Walk-Through protocol?*

When schools begin using the Walk-Through protocol they are often surprised to discover that it meets them exactly where they are. In situations where trusting relationships are the norm and where professional inquiry is already part of the culture, the protocol becomes just another useful tool to help the school get better at its work. However, many schools find themselves in need of a tool that will help them build trust. The Walk-Through protocol keeps them safe as trust grows. Because it is a positive process, there is no need to eliminate failure before beginning to succeed.

For schools whose professional development culture has been more didactic than inquiring, the protocol provides a safe haven in which to rediscover that **inquiry drives improvement**—to learn that they do have time to learn together because what they learn together results in significantly better student learning and achievement.

Some schools find themselves with a preponderance of novice teachers, and wonder how the protocol can work in their situation. Part of the Walk-Through protocol's magic is that it supports new and experienced educators as they learn together. In fact, teachers with many years of service often comment that the innocent questions asked by novice teachers have caused them to question practices they have used for years—they have learned something by questioning their own established practices. All teachers mention that the opportunity to be in each other's classrooms is a wonderful professional learning opportunity.

Finally, the Walk-Through protocol creates an environment where professionals can begin to ask questions about the very beliefs that form the basis of their practice. Logic tells us that current results derive from current practice. To get better results, we must believe that altering practice is necessary, and then we must make changes that make a difference in student learning in the moment and over time.

### How do administrators participate?

It is important to emphasize that this is *not* an evaluation process. Evaluation and supervision are important aspects of an administrator's role, of course, and they do not go away in schools that adopt the Walk-Through protocol.

Administrators play a critical role in championing and endorsing the process, and they assure the organizational support that is needed. But they also have to be willing to be the quiet partner in the process—to step back and let this be a teacher-led activity. Administrators have to trust and value what teachers see.

The question of when, and if, administrators participate as members of a Walk-Through team is one that needs to be worked through by each school. As schools embark on this journey, administrators may find that trust builds more easily if teachers can initially work only with their peers. Some participants have to engage in the process before they believe it is non-evaluative. As one principal put it, "We just naturally go to evaluating something, to say this is good or bad. This practice absolutely demands that doesn't happen. We must talk about what we actually see, and we must talk to one another so it becomes clear what we are doing and how we can get better."

### *Why the Walk-Through protocol works*

In most protocols, we bring a piece of student work to the professional table. In the Walk-Through protocol we gather the professionals around the student table. We improve our practice by concentrating on what we observe as students are learning. We bring students and teachers, practice and results, into the same picture at the same time. We measure our progress by student success, and we do it with consistency—together.

# Chapter 2.  Nuts and Bolts of the SMP Walk-Through Protocol

"The SMP Walk-Through protocol transformed my thinking. I used to believe that good teaching could be discovered by observing what teachers do. Now I know that good teaching is discovered by observing what students learn."—Instructional Coach, Antelope Valley Union High School District, California

School leaders search for effective and practical ways to live out what research tells us makes a difference in student learning. Research literature is easy to embrace theoretically. It is much more difficult to turn research into compelling collective action. How do we create the climate where the trusting members of a "professional learning community" improve the results of their practice? What does it take to be the "small learning community" that includes students and parents as well as professional educators? What will WE do to harness the positive power of "community" to transform the learning and achievement of all students?

This Walk-Through protocol provides both a process and a tool for inquiry-based professional development, community engagement, and ultimately student self-direction. It starts with a school's commitment to build an inquiry model that assumes the capacity for extraordinary learning on the part of students, teachers, administrators, and families. The protocol can be employed narrowly—to guide the improving practice of a couple of teachers with a passion for biology, for example—or more broadly. Many of the improving schools highlighted in the chapters that follow chose the Walk-Through protocol as a frame for school-wide professional development that led to exceptional growth in learning and student achievement. When fully developed, the protocol includes families and students, as well as educators. This creates a community where all members approach learning as an inquiry and proactively design their success.

This "Nuts and Bolts" chapter provides a road map for your journey, by outlining the specific steps of the Walk-Through protocol.

### *Why a protocol for walking through classrooms?*

Classroom visits or observations have long been a standard part of educational practice. Combining visits or observations with a carefully crafted protocol that defines HOW we will visit and WHAT we will do with our observations creates comfort with the process and helps assure that something purposeful will result.

Protocols are defined as "accepted or established codes of procedures or behaviors in any group, organization or situation." They are used to structure conversations by putting unpredictable results into a predictable frame. The predictable frame guides the conversation through a series of steps that are consistent and known in advance to all participants. The predictable frame sets time limits and structures activities so there is a beginning, middle, and end to each conversation.

Protocols give everyone a chance to participate by deliberately creating space for all voices. The structure fosters reflection, dialogue and the type of questioning essential to the cycle of inquiry introduced in the previous chapter.

## *What is the protocol?*

This Walk-Through protocol provides a consistent process for engaging in classroom observations and establishes safe, non-judgmental norms for talking and planning collectively based on the data derived from the observations. The protocol has three components:

1. **Before** the walk—a time for preparation where participants agree on norms and a focus question.
2. **During** the walk—a time to collect evidence of students engaged in their own learning.
3. **After** the walk—a time to explore together the evidence collected, reflect on its meaning, and decide on next steps.

## *Before the walk*

Part of the preparation for the Walk-Through is building the context where collecting observable data in classrooms is the next, most useful step in a school's inquiry into effective practices that work for students. By looking at the evidence of student understanding, participation and interaction—the results of our teaching—the protocol ensures our collaborative focus stays on student achievement, rather than becoming an evaluation of teacher instruction. Many schools that are already engaged in initiatives to improve student learning—schools with established settings and ways of learning together, planning next steps and assessing their efficacy—have created a natural context for initiating the Walk-Through protocol. Schools where the concept of a learning community is new might need to spend some time building understanding of an inquiry cycle sustained by community members who are learning together.

We recommend that you begin your work with an explicit opportunity for your staff to learn the nuts and bolts, ask questions, and practice using the protocol. Refer to the appendix for sample agendas and timeframes that you might tailor to your own specific needs.

When groups agree beforehand on a set of ground rules, or norms, that will guide their actions and discussions, it is easier to have productive, honest conversations. Throughout this chapter (and others) we will introduce guidelines specific to this protocol. In addition, we recommend that your school community participate in a norms-setting process that establishes the guidelines for conversation that meet the needs of your site.

As an example, the "norms" below have been developed and used internally by SMP staff.

**LISTEN**

**Intend to understand rather than respond or persuade.**

**INVITE DIFFERENCES**

**Move away from either/or. Embrace "and".**

**SUSPEND YOUR ASSUMPTIONS**

**Make your assumptions visible to yourself and others. Then, be less sure that those assumptions are right.**

**SPEAK FROM AWARNESS**

**Be honest with yourself about your purpose and intent in speaking.**

**ASSUME GOODWILL**

**Listen without judging the other person's intentions. Assume their intentions are the very best.**

If your school has already established norms, of course you will continue to use them. Should your school not have done so, we highly recommend that you engage in this community-building process prior to initiating classroom walk-throughs. A group activity to develop norms is included in the appendix.

Sometime before the actual classroom visits, participants develop a Walk-Through focus question that will help them explore an important aspect of student learning in their classrooms. Focus questions often emerge during the implementation of new programs or initiatives.

For example, after receiving and reviewing the results of their state assessments, the faculty at one middle school committed to providing their students with strategies that would help them read better by increasing their comprehension skills. The entire staff attended a workshop on specific and explicit strategies to increase reading comprehension for students.

Teachers integrated the new strategies into their instructional practice. At the end of two weeks they wondered what difference the strategies were making for students, and chose to focus their Walk-Through with the question *What evidence do we see that students use explicit strategies to make sense of text?* They were not looking to check on **whether** students were doing what they were "supposed to be doing," but instead looking to understand **how** and **if** students were making use of the new strategies to intentionally support their own understanding of text.

Many schools find the focus for their walk-throughs by exploring the improvement initiatives already underway at their site and in their district. We have found it useful to employ a simple T-Chart (like the one pictured in Figure 1) to help schools connect multiple efforts to explicit student outcomes.

## Figure 1. T-Chart used to develop a focus question

**What school initiatives are you currently implementing that have a direct bearing on your professional practice and student learning?**

| Current Initiatives | Expected student outcomes |
|---|---|
| Comprehensive School Reform Program—A three year school-wide plan to address low student achievement | Students meet NCLB progress requirements on mandated tests for standards mastery |
| Single School Plan—A consolidated plan for the integration of Title I and other categorical funds and activities in support of entitled students | Student mastery of standards |
| Scottish Storyline | Student mastery of standards through student-created narrative |
| Guided Language Development Design | Mastery of content and skills standards by students who are English learners |
| Intervention | Differentiated support for students not yet meeting proficiency on standards measures |
| Open Court Reading<br>  Primary grades<br>  Upper grades | Student competency in reading through direct instruction |
| Carousel of Ideas | Mastery of content and skills standards by students who are English learners |

When this T-chart was used as a graphic organizer, teachers realized that multi-faceted initiatives from the state, the district, and the school itself had at their core congruent student outcomes. In this school's case, student outcomes focused around increasing student fluency in using the English language for both conversational and academic purposes, and applying that fluency in both written and oral formats. Once identified, these specific outcomes suggested a productive focus question: **What evidence do we see that students are speaking, reading, and writing to learn in English?**

### *Walk-Throughs in Practice* ...

On any given day at the Armstrong Middle School in Rhode Island you would see students reading, or at least appearing to read. The library's open door policy invites students to drop in whenever they want. Most classrooms have comfortable areas for reading, and are well stocked with books.

Yet in spite of the print-rich and literacy-friendly environment, state assessments continued to indicate low levels of comprehension for most students, particularly when working with non-fiction text. The faculty at Armstrong decided they needed to learn more about the "during reading" strategies that would help their students comprehend more of what they were reading, and they knew their experience using Walk-Throughs would help.

As part of their professional development, the 6th grade English Language Arts team read <u>When Kids Can't Read, What Teachers Can Do</u> by Kylene Beers. They were particularly interested in the "Say Something" strategy and decided to try it out in their own classrooms. This strategy is described by Beers (p. 105):

*"Say Something is a very simple strategy that interrupts a student's reading of a text; giving her a chance to think about what she is reading. Students get into groups of two or three and take turns reading a portion of a text aloud. As they read, they occasionally pause to 'say something' about what was read. They make a prediction, ask a question, clarify a confusion, comment on what's happening, or connect what's in the text to something they know. The reading partners offer a response to what was said, then a different student continues the reading until the next time they pause to say something."*

The team was excited and believed this strategy could make a difference with their students. Once they were comfortable with the practice, they began modeling "Say Something" in their own classrooms, and then explaining the procedure to their students. Two or three times a week they structured reading groups to follow this new process.

After a month of using this practice in their classrooms, the team began planning their next Walk-Through. Everyone was curious to know how and if the "Say Something" strategy might be making a difference with their students. They really hoped that students had internalized this strategy and were using it on their own. They certainly didn't want to wait for the next cycle of state assessments to see if it comprehension was improving!

The group shared a number of ideas, and finally settled on a focus question:

**What evidence do we see that students are talking with one another to make sense of what they are reading?**

This focus question was shared with all faculty members at Armstrong before the Walk-Through, and most teachers welcomed the team into their rooms. The team visited each other's classrooms, and also some of the math, science, and social studies classes to see if students were using the strategy to help them make better sense of text in all content areas.

# Effective Focus Questions

## Who Participates in the Walk-Through?

*The Walk-Through protocol has an especially high impact when teachers walk. This is because the process is designed to examine the links between teacher practice and student learning. The composition of walking teams is often determined by what the school community wants from the experience.*

*There are two roles for teachers in the Walk-Through protocol: teachers participate as members of a Walk-Through team, and teachers participate by opening their classrooms for observation.*

*Involving the wider school community in walk-throughs can bring unique lenses and voices to the process, and expansion to the wider school community is a useful goal.*

Effective focus questions are often phrased as "What evidence do we see (or hear) that students . . . ?" A question is effective if:

- It emerges from the natural curiosity of teachers themselves;
- It focuses on what students are doing;
- It is open-ended enough to allow possibilities to emerge—it does not have one "right" answer;
- It is about discovering, rather than measuring;
- It can be answered by describing what is observed; and
- It generates data that will provide information about progress toward the stated goal.

## The day of the Walk-Through

The participants meet together in a conference room, classroom, or library. The Walk-Through coordinator arranges and distributes the schedule for classroom observations with a copy of the day's focus question. Participants should review the schedule and make sure they have the forms for collecting their observations. It is helpful to provide clipboards, so that participants can easily record their observations during the Walk-Through.

This is also the time to develop (or review) agreements for walking through classrooms. These should include:

- The number of adults in any one classroom at any one time (we recommend five or fewer as a manageable group)
- When and how observers may speak to students (for example, we do not interrupt students during a directed lesson and generally ask the teacher's permission during other activities)
- Whether observers write notes in the classroom or in the hallway
- When and how observers examine student work in the classroom (for example, writing folders or student portfolios)

## During the visit

Participants form small groups of five or fewer observers. Teams set out with a schedule, school map, and observation recording forms. Visitors spend five to seven minutes in each classroom. Groups select one member as the timekeeper and another to facilitate "outside the door" conversations. Roles can rotate as participants increase their level of comfort with the process.

Observers visit the classrooms to collect evidence in relation to the focus question. Observers pay attention to what students are doing, the work products that are displayed, interactions between teacher and students, and student interactions with each other. Observers may ask questions of the students, provided that students are working in such a way that the questioning is not a distraction. Observers should make note of any student work outside of the classroom (bulletin boards, display cases) that relate to the focus question.

Observers are challenged to act "like a video camera" and record only things that they actually see and hear. The observation graphic (see Figure 2.) is used to collect the evidence—without interpretation. It is important to note that teacher names and room numbers are purposely left off the observation graphic.

> **Why five to seven minutes?**
>
> We have found observing many classrooms for short periods of time allows us to gather accurate evidence of student learning as it relates to the focus question.

# Figure 2. The observation graphic

*Classroom Walk-Throughs Graphic Organizer*

Date _____5/23_____ Subject __Science_____ Grade Level _2____

Focus Question: _____
What evidence do we see or hear that students are speaking, reading, and writing to learn English?

| OBSERVATIONS | NOTES, THOUGHTS, AND QUESTIONS |
|---|---|
| Small groups of 5 students talking to one another as they examined different kinds of seeds—pointing out different features | I wonder how often students work in small groups? How often do they have science? |
| One student working alone holding a seed and looking at it with a magnifying glass | I wonder how students were grouped for this project? |
| 3 students using a worksheet to lit different characteristics of seeds—color, shape, markings, etc. Comparing answers and trying to agree on correct answer | |
| Two students working together—one is using the magnifying glass to show me and explain a small mark on one seed | |
| Two students sitting in back of room quietly using their text books to complete a worksheet—using the text and dictionary to define words | |
| Student made posters on the wall related to science—the water cycle, climate zones | |

## Outside the door sharing

After each classroom visit the observation partners jot down or add to their notes, and then talk for three minutes (away from the classroom) about what they have just heard and seen related to the focus area. This is a sharing of evidence, rather than a conversation.

Part of the reason for the outside-the-door sharing is that participants will see, record, and share different observations. This conversation is not judgmental, and should focus on evidence that has been observed. Observers might start off by saying, "I saw ..." or "I heard ...." Think of this process as being similar to a Socratic Seminar, where participants are continually referring to the text to support their comments. In this case, the classroom visit is the "text."

The facilitator ensures that sharing concentrates on evidence of student learning and is related to the focus question. The facilitator takes responsibility for including each member of the team at this stage. "round robin" process, where each person shares observations, is particularly effective.

Teams of observers repeat this process outside each of their scheduled classrooms. All the groups reconvene at an agreed-upon time and place to engage in the debrief portion of the protocol.

*Facilitator's Tip:*

*The outside the door sharing provides an opportunity for teams to "practice" recording observable evidence. Often during the first few rounds it is necessary for the facilitator to remind the group that they are not sharing opinions about what they see. Additionally, this is not the time to note what was NOT observed, or what you assumed you might see.*

## After the walk

After all the observers have completed the classroom visits, they reconvene to debrief. Sometimes schools find it convenient to schedule the debriefing after school—or even a day later. It is appropriate to invite the teachers who have been visited to observe the debrief.

There are specific timed guidelines for conducting the debrief:

Introduce debrief guidelines (2 minutes)
Share and chart observations (8 minutes)
Identify patterns and trends (8 minutes)
Chart questions about patterns and trends (7 minutes)
Determine and chart next steps (7 minutes)
Reflect on the debrief process (3 minutes)

*Facilitator's Tip:*

*The timing for each of the rounds may be adjusted. It is helpful if the facilitator reviews each step of the process with the group before starting.*

The debrief process works most effectively with fifteen to twenty people. If the group is larger than that, it is helpful to debrief in two groups. All participants who walked or "observed classrooms" sit in a circle (or semi-circle) so everyone can hear and see each other easily. The room should be set up with two charts for collecting evidence and notes, along with markers and tape.

*Facilitator's Tip:*

*We find it helpful to have recorders use dark markers to chart – and even more helpful if they use two alternating, contrasting colors. This makes it simple for everyone in the room to follow along and read without eyestrain.*

The Walk-Through coordinator may facilitate the debrief, or may ask for another volunteer. Two volunteer recorders alternate in capturing evidence shared by participants (two recorders allow the charting to keep up with a natural conversation flow).

The facilitator may suggest the group take five minutes to review their notes, identify a few key observations they would like to share, and formulate a question or questions that they are wondering about as a result of the visits.

The facilitator introduces the debrief process, and reviews the steps. Participants are reminded of the established group norms, and referred to the charted focus question. Participants may "pass" at any time. No teacher names or room numbers are used during the debrief process.

## Sharing Evidence, Observations, and Patterns

In round-robin style, participants share one observation related to the Focus Question. Only evidence (not lack of) is presented, using literal description to respond to "What did you see or hear?" For example, "I saw students answering questions." Rounds continue until all observations are shared or time is called.

Participants individually review the charted observations, and then work in pairs or triads to identify (and support with evidence) patterns within the data. Patterns are recorded on a new sheet of chart paper.

The next section of the debrief process is devoted to raising and sharing questions that arise from the pattern identification. Some questions may be easily answered—for example, you could find out how students were grouped for activities in a classroom by asking the teacher. We call these clarifying questions.

Other questions are more open-ended, and less easily answered. They often express things you wonder about. For example: "*I wonder how our students who are learning English use the experience of working in groups to extend their command of academic language?*" We call these probing questions—and the group discussion of these often leads to the next, most important area for professional development, learning and data collection.

An effective way to surface important questions is to have participants talk again in pairs or triads, about the questions that come up for them as they think about identified patterns. The facilitator can then ask each group to share one or two questions. These questions are charted as they are shared.

## Next Steps

The facilitator takes responsibility for moving the conversation into a dialogue on next steps. Sometimes groups are tempted to use quick methods for organizing their observations, and leap immediately to solutions. We have found that the single most important moment in the debrief process comes when patterns and the questions about them are considered in open dialogue. When we move beyond the "first, quick answers" that grow out of our current assumptions, we begin to explore the deeper, more complex interrelationships that will make the difference for improved adult and student learning and transformed results.

 *Facilitator's Tip:*

*There are a number of simple ways to help your group move toward consensus on next steps.*

*In either round-robin structure or informal sharing, ideas for next steps are shared and charters.*

*Using colored dots or check marks, have members of the group select three areas that they "want to know more about" or "want to see more of."*

*A sample guide for determining next steps is included in the appendix.*

An important outcome of this dialogue will be the sharing of many possible next steps. The facilitator has the delicate task of moving the group from open-ended conversation of many possibilities to consensus around one agreed-upon next step. Next steps may grow out of identified patterns that you want to see more evidence of next time you walk.

Next steps might include professional reading and learning together, sharing expertise and choosing a best practice to implement, and visiting other school sites. "Next steps" culminate in a collective commitment to do something differently that you expect to be more effective with students—a change in professional practice.

Before the group leaves, a date should be set for the next Walk-Through. Groups often find it useful to begin to frame their next focus question at this time. Consideration must be given to accomplishing the "next steps" the group has laid out prior to the next meeting, so that the next Walk-Through can yield evidence of the effectiveness of the steps you have taken.

Because this activity is a reflective process, it ends with an opportunity to think and write about the experience, to enable the group to grow in its effectiveness. One way to structure this reflection is to have participants jot down a few thoughts about these prompts:

*Something I noticed about myself was …*
*Something I noticed about the group was …*
*Something I noticed about the facilitation was …*
*Something I noticed about the process was …*

As a closing activity, the facilitator asks participants to round-robin share just one of these items.

## Sharing with the Staff

Evidence, patterns, questions, and next steps generated by the Walk-Through team are shared with staff. There are several effective ways to accomplish this. All staff might be invited to listen in on the Walk-Through team debrief. Another useful method is to have members of the Walk-Through team act as liaisons to their grade levels or departments.

Typing up notes and distributing them may not be the best way to engage and inform other staff. BUT leaving the "raw" charts posted in a place where people are likely to see them frequently creates curiosity that may lead to useful conversations.

You will decide what the best method is for your own school. The important part is that staff knows they are invited to participate and that the process remains open and inclusive.

> "At our school, a big obstacle to improvement was turning planning into action. Now, because we use a monthly protocol for observing, finding patterns in what we saw, and planning next steps, the action is built in. We are on our way to higher student achievement!"—Teacher, Fremont Elementary School, Santa Ana Unified School District, California

# Chapter 3. Walk-Throughs as a Catalyst for School Improvement

**Connecting curriculum, instruction, and assessment through a teacher-driven cycle of improvement**

> "We always knew our students were capable of high achievement, but until we linked our Walk-Through data with teacher collaboration and professional development, our results didn't begin to match our expectations."—Literacy Coach, Miramonte Elementary School, Mountain View School District, El Monte, CA

Curriculum, instruction, assessment, and professional development are the traditional legs of the academic stool. As a profession we have grown more skilled in these areas, and we are getting better at defining discrete efforts with the potential to support improvement extremely well. But this approach is inherently limited by educator and school power to control opportunities beyond the classroom and school. These efforts, by themselves, cannot create the conditions that are necessary for truly transformational growth in student achievement.

Academic content standards, clear descriptions of *what students should know and be able to do*, are present in virtually every school. Curriculum experts carefully match materials to defined benchmarks and pacing guides for each classroom. Instructional specialists work with teachers to provide training, support, and coaching in how to use these materials to deliver the curriculum to the student. Assessment professionals design tasks and tests that measure the end product—how close students are to achieving those standards. We measure the gap between our expectations of student knowledge and actual student knowledge of those standards very carefully. We deliver that "gap" information back to the system that created it and ask the system to close the gap.

But, as Albert Einstein reminded us, "We can't solve problems by using the same kind of thinking we used when we created them." Solutions provided in a top-down fashion, often delivered by outside experts, can create incremental improvements for a period of time. However they cannot foster the kind of transformational change we need in schooling today.

Solution framers in education often strive to apply linear cause-and-effect thinking to create simple, easy-to-implement solutions. Thus, it is no surprise that solutions often require fixing the teacher (through some trainable process) to fix the problem. The demands of accountability, combined with solutions generated by outsiders, move the locus of control for instruction even further away from the classroom. Yet the most powerful leverage point is at the intersection between the student, the teacher, and the content.

Walk-Throughs strike at this leverage point, and enable teachers to get to the heart of what students are doing and understanding in a different and holistic way. The protocol works because it is based on teachers' own questions about student learning—it builds on teachers' desires to become better teachers. Through conversations with colleagues, focused talk about individual teaching experiences becomes shared learning about effective instruction. Successful participation in these productive professional conversations increases the capacity of the group to be a professional learning community—that safe place to ask hard questions about the links between results, content, and teacher practice. The Walk-Through protocol is a tool that a learning community can use to deepen its collective understanding of instruction, moving beyond identifying and fixing problems to identifying and enhancing student mastery of content and skills.

No amount of data or understanding will, by itself, move a system toward improvement in a purposeful way. The energy and knowledge generated by Walk-Throughs needs to be channeled into *doing something* and constantly comparing the results from what you are doing to the results you hope to achieve. That is the heart of continuous improvement.

*Using the Walk-Through to drive a cycle of continuous improvement*

The evidence collected as part of a Walk-Through can drive a cycle of improvement by *focusing on the effects of instruction*. Most schools are fairly skilled at collecting and analyzing student assessment data, providing them with useful information about student content knowledge. Most schools are also fairly skilled at choosing curricula and instructional programs that will "deliver" the appropriate content to all students. What is missing, however, is the opportunity to *observe first-hand the effects of the delivered program on students*. While we are comprehensive in our efforts to ensure teachers are "doing it right" and delivering curricular programs with fidelity, we have no formal method of ensuring we are "doing the right thing" by reflecting on how students are understanding and embracing both the content and skills we want them to master.

We all use continuous improvement as a process in our daily lives to achieve goals that are meaningful to us. Think about how you chose your undergraduate college. You probably read a few things about the best colleges out there, and while *Newsweek* or the *Peterson Guide* may have informed your decision, they didn't make the choice for you. You created your own desired future by putting some thought into what careers you were interested in, or how close or far away from home you wanted to be, or what you had heard from friends or relatives, or even where you thought you had a chance of getting in. You gathered data on possible schools; maybe you even conducted your own Walk-Through by visiting the school and talking to current students.

Likewise, most of us employ *some* elements of this cycle in thinking about professional goals that are important to us. The chart (see page 48) illustrates what we believe to be the *important elements* in a cycle of improvement—and we suggest this as a way to formalize or structure your discussions about moving your "next steps" into reality and incorporating meaningful, positive changes into the daily practice and culture of your school.

*Define a desired future*. Clearly defining and stating a "desired future" is a powerful way of describing what your students are capable of achieving. It allows you to visualize and describe success. It makes a statement about what is important to you as an individual, as a member of a grade-level or content team, or as a member of a larger educational community.

It can be surprisingly difficult to find words to describe what you actually see as a desired future for students. School vision and mission statements can be helpful in the broad sense—here you might find a statement like, "all students will be productive members of society and lifelong learners." But what does that mean in your classroom? What skill or trait does that demand from your students?

Sometimes the results of large-scale assessments suggest a desired future for you. In this case, your school may have established a goal such as "All students will apply basic computational skills effectively to solve mathematics problems." Your desired future might be even more specific than that—you and your grade-level colleagues might be struggling to implement a new writing program, and your desired future might be that all your students write a compelling five paragraph persuasive essay by the end of the second semester.

These examples all serve the purpose of providing a direction for your work—in effect by keeping your goal in sight and in mind as you engage in your day-to-day activities. You probably have several desired futures in mind at any given time, though all should be aligned with the overall direction and goals of your school.

# Walk-Throughs as part of a Cycle of Improvement

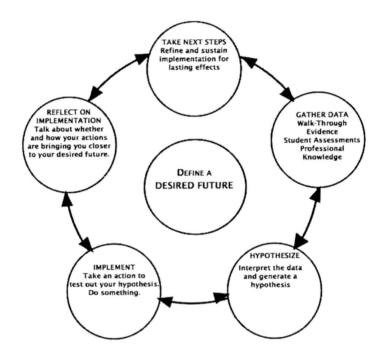

*Gather data.* Before you can move effectively toward your desired future, you need a firm understanding of where you are. Gathering data helps you describe and understand your current reality. Materials from state assessments, district benchmarks, classroom work, and teacher professional knowledge are all important contributors. Evidence gathered from a Walk-Through is particularly valuable at this stage, because it is often the only data you have that emerges from a systematic and formal process that is rooted in observing evidence of some aspect of students as they are actually engaged in their work.

We tend to think of *data* as something that is gathered to *answer* a question. However, when we work in an environment of continuous improvement, data it is more likely to *create more questions*. The evidence collected during a Walk-Through and the patterns that are identified often suggest ideas about how to improve practice and move closer to your desired future. All too frequently we stop at this point, believing data has provided us with an answer. In truth, it has only suggested some *possible* answers.

*Hypothesize*. In the cycle of improvement model, this is the time to structure your ideas about different ways of working that *might* have a positive influence on the behavior or outcome you are trying to change. It is critically important that you actually tie this idea to the positive behavior or result you hope it will cause, and that the idea arises from a collaborative discussion of the data you have generated and the questions it raises. For example, a first look at data might suggest that students are not clear that math problems can be solved using multiple approaches or methods. You might *hypothesize* that working with math manipulatives will lead to students who understand and employ multiple methods to solving problems, and that an important next step is to increase teacher comfort and capacity in teaching with manipulatives.

*Implement.* Here is the opportunity to actually test out your hypothesis by doing something in a coordinated, collaborative fashion. In the example above, you and your group might decide to read and discuss a book together (like Marilyn Burns' *10 Big Math*

*Ideas*), trying out a few of the suggested activities in the classroom. Remember this is an inquiry, you are trying out a *possible solution* at this point, *not implementing a known solution.* Colleagues might be encouraged to try different activities, in different ways, with different groups of students.

*Reflect on implementation.* Time and settings to reflect on what has been implemented are deliberately built into the improvement process. It is the time to share successful strategies for implementation, certainly, but also to reflect on your original hypothesis and see if you still believe you are on the right track toward your desired future. This may be an appropriate time to plan another Walk-Through to gather additional evidence, making your reflection process richer and more student-based. It is very likely that you will find yourself going back and forth between the implementation and reflection steps in an iterative process until you find yourself with something that works, something that appears to be moving you closer to your desired future. This "little victory" should be acknowledged, appreciated, and shared.

*Next steps.* Your "small experiment" in changing practice has been tried, probably in different ways with different people, and you have had the chance to reflect on implementation as well as to gather evidence on how these changes are affecting students in your classroom. You may decide you are on the wrong track—and it is time to go back and create another hypothesis. More often, you have learned something fundamentally important about delivering instruction in your classroom (your little victory) and it is time to search for ways to share the good news with your teacher and administrator colleagues. This is your opportunity to make recommendations and advocate for changing practice—and to have a real effect on the culture and efficacy of your school.

## *Building on and sustaining positive change*

Today, many teachers struggle with a sense that they lack control over the things they do in the classroom. Curriculum and program materials are prescribed. Pacing guides seek to align daily lessons across classrooms, schools, and even districts. Finally, benchmark assessments, district assessments and state assessments are required at defined times each year, often with much elapsed time between administration of assessments and teacher receipt of quantified results.

Yet teachers do retain a fair degree of control over how they deliver instruction, use the results of mandated assessments, and work with students on a day-to-day basis. Improving instructional practice can be the key leverage point for improving student achievement. Teachers who participate in Walk-Throughs and the resulting professional discussions learn from one another, certainly, but also make important discoveries about their own practice, how their students are engaged in learning, and the connection between the two. By focusing on evidence of student learning, teachers have the opportunity to implement necessary instructional changes thoughtfully, with a clear understanding of the difference they expect to see in student work.

While the Walk-Through process has the most immediate impact on instruction, it also informs curriculum, assessment, and professional development. The data collected on a "walk" can provide evidence about what's working at the classroom level. This evidence can be used by schools and districts to re-examine curriculum, develop alternative assess-ments, and as a foundation for cohesive district-wide professional development. This process of "managing up" gives classroom teachers an opportunity to be part of the school and district's continuous improve-ment cycle by connecting policy and program deci-sions to their observable effect on student learning.

**Walk-Throughs in Practice ...**

*Defining a Desired Future.*
After looking at the results of state testing in Spring 2005, teachers at Miramonte Elementary School (Mountain View School District, El Monte, California) were searching for ways to improve the academic performance of their students, particularly English Learners. Miramonte teachers and administrators envisioned all students, including their EL's as able users of the English language for a range of purposes and audiences, including the use of academic language to understand the standards-based curriculum.

*Gathering data.* A picture of "current reality" began to emerge when the Miramonte faculty analyzed state testing data. They felt a need to gain a deeper understanding of what was happening in classrooms. They had been working diligently to learn new instructional strategies, but believed that they needed a closer view and real-time data about what students were learning and understanding. A team attended UCLA SMP's Walk-Through Institute and was enthusiastic about trying this non-evaluative process to observe what students were doing. They developed the focus question, "What evidence do we see that students are actively engaged in their learning?" After introducing the Walk-Through process to their faculty, they implemented Walk-Throughs during their one-hour weekly grade-level planning times, visiting classrooms across the grade levels. The faculty then gathered to review the collected observation data, identify patterns and trends, and ask questions based on the themes that emerged.

*Hypothesize.* Teachers hypothesized that giving students more opportunities to speak and listen for understanding in the classroom would help them to connect to prior experience, and thus build the academic vocabulary required to understand rigorous content.

*Implement.* Teachers decided to take action on several fronts, including sharing instructional strategies to promote speaking and listening; comparing the six-week benchmark assessment language arts results with what they had observed students doing in classrooms; and trying a test-thinking strategy that encouraged students to dialogue with a partner or small group about how they solved a problem and chose a test answer.

*Reflect on Implementation.* Teachers scheduled another Walk-Through to provide themselves with early feedback on the effects of the new strategies they were implementing. They found that students were actively working in groups; sorting content vocabulary according to attributes with much debate and discussion, collaboratively writing stories and building on each other's thoughts, and using a pair share "test-thinking" strategy to compare answers and solve problems. Teachers were able to connect generalized data about how students were doing on state and benchmark assessments with observational data about how students were engaged in using the basic skills of listening and speaking to build capacity in language fluency, academic vocabulary, and comprehension.

*Next Steps.* Teachers decided to focus their grade level meetings on interpreting data to establish priorities, examining curriculum to exchange ideas and align efforts, and sharing strategies that promoted language development in the content areas.

It was a bumpy journey at times, full of questions, fraught with ongoing logistical and time constraints. After receiving Spring 2006 California Standards Test results, teachers, administrators, parents, and students celebrated Miramonte's substantial achievement in *exceeding* state and national proficiency levels and academic targets in English/Language Arts and Math for *all* student subgroups, including English Learners. Walk-Throughs tied to a teacher-driven Cycle of Improvement provided a protocol and tool for focusing the school community's efforts in moving toward their desired future for students, propelled by teachers' own questions and observations.

# Chapter 4. Using Walk-Through Protocols to Sustain a Professional Learning Community

## The Six to Six Magnet School

"Teachers need scaffolds and bridges to improve, just like students do. That's what the Walk-Through process has done for us ... it has given us the strategies and structure to help one another become better teachers."—Classroom teacher, Six to Six Magnet School, Bridgeport, CT

It is interesting to hear how many teachers at Six to Six talk about the Walk-Through process using a bridge metaphor. The campus is composed of two buildings—one for the elementary grades and one for the middle grades—with an indoor walkway  between the two sites. In the past, this walkway was a real barrier between two separate and isolated cultures. Introducing and practicing Walk-Throughs has brought the faculty together in a culture of learning: teachers now "cross the bridge" every day.

## The setting

Bridgeport, Connecticut, is home to the Six to Six Interdistrict Magnet School, a public school serving 400 students in grades PK-8, with a staff of 55 adults (40 faculty). The Six to Six complex includes an elementary program and the Thurgood Marshall Middle School. The school serves students and their families from 6 am until 6 pm each day.

Known widely as the 'Park City,' Bridgeport is Connecticut's largest city. Bridgeport combines the rich history of a powerful industrial center with a stunning diversity of people and their cultures.

Interdistrict magnets were established in the state of Connecticut as a means of reducing the racial and economic stratification across schools and communities. Six to Six draws students from the communities of Bridgeport, Fairfield, Stratford and Trumbull – communities that mirror the diversity of the state. New students are selected by lottery each spring based on established demographic targets.

| Current school enrollments by gender/ethnicity | |
|---|---:|
| American Indian/Alaskan | 2 |
| Asian/Pacific Islander | 12 |
| Black | 144 |
| Caucasian | 140 |
| Hispanic | 111 |
| Female | 207 |
| Male | 202 |
| TOTAL ENROLLMENT | 409 |

As a *Title I* school, all the students at Six to Six are considered economically disadvantaged. Students in grades 4, 6 and 8 participate in the state-mandated Connecticut Mastery Test (CMT), used as the basis for determining Adequate Yearly Progress. Based on the results of the Spring 2006 testing, Six to Six achieved their whole-school academic proficiency targets in both reading and math, as well as achieving their sub-group targets for Caucasians and Hispanics (in both reading and math) and Economically Disadvantaged students (in mathematics). The faculty is using Walk-Throughs to help them support student subgroups in meeting all growth targets.

Six to Six is part of the *Cooperative Education Services* (CES) district – a regional education service center chartered by the state and serving southwestern Connecticut. The School Planning and Management Team (SPMT) makes decisions at the school level. This team is made up of families, staff and administrators. The school also has a Board of Trustees representing five partner districts. This Board approves policy for the school.

Six to Six Interdistrict Magnet School
601 Pearl Harbor Street
Bridgeport, Connecticut 06610
Telephone 203.330.6775
Website http://www.ces.k12.ct.us/page.cfm?p=21

Chris LaBelle, Principal
Robyn Proto, Assistant Principal
Howard Hornreich, Assistant Principal

## The mission and goals

*The shared mission of the staff and families of the Six to Six Interdistrict Magnet school is to foster educational excellence and lifelong learning in an atmosphere that honors each child's physical, intellectual, social and emotional needs within a diverse school community based on mutual respect and a sense of social conscience.*

Growing out of this mission statement, the Six to Six community has created five comprehensive school goals to guide their development through 2008:

1. To improve student achievement in reading for specific subgroups identified as not meeting AYP.
2. To improve student achievement in mathematics.
3. To improve student achievement in science.
4. To establish a process of teacher collaboration focused on increasing student learning and school climate.
5. To increase funding for Six to Six.

## Using the protocol to create a community

Principal Chris LaBelle joined the staff of Six to Six in 2004. At that time, the school was in the final year of a three-year Comprehensive School Reform grant, focused on improving literacy. The grant had provided funding for rich and plentiful professional development around literacy and math instruction in the middle elementary grades – delivered largely through outside consultants. Teachers were beginning to implement new reading, writing and mathematics approaches and programs in their classrooms. At faculty and grade level meetings, they were talking about how the programs were working in their classrooms.

Yet LaBelle saw and heard evidence of a fractured, isolated faculty. The physical walkway between the middle and elementary schools served as a barrier rather than a bridge – with a sense at the middle school of being 'have-nots' while their elementary school colleagues reaped the benefits of CSR. Teachers at the elementary level were struggling to implement new ideas and ways of teaching individually in their own classrooms, without any way to learn from and support one another.

Vague ideas about 'professional learning communities' were starting to surface in the school. Teachers were approaching administrators individually and asking if they could visit another classroom – "Can I see something else? Someone else?" When the opportunity to attend a Walk-Through training presented itself, the administrators seized it as a way not only to keep the conversation going, but to deepen and expand it across the entire faculty. In LaBelle's words, "At the time, I was very interested in PLCs and believed in their power. As an administrator, the work of the school appeared fragmented, with everyone in a different place. The Walk-Through training landed in my lap and I fused the two together, thinking it might be a simpler, quicker process for the faculty."

## The first six months

Principal LaBelle, Assistant Principal Robyn Proto, and four classroom teachers attended SMP's first east coast *Walk-Through* training in Providence, Rhode Island (November 2005). As part of the training, the team spent two days visiting schools using a focus question: *What evidence do we see of students engaged in their own learning*? While learning the protocol, the team realized this was a powerful process to use back at Six to Six – a process that might quickly propel the faculty into establishing the culture of collaboration that was both wanted and needed.

The Six to Six team spent a number of hours discussing and debating the best way to bring this back and arrived at a plan that was as unique as the school itself. The essence was both powerful and simple – they wanted to allow ALL staff to participate in a non-threatening way and discover the power of the protocol for themselves. Knowing that trust was the cornerstone of successful collaboration, their design *made* the time to allow that trust to evolve into a solid foundation.

Starting in December of 2005, the Walk-Through team scheduled walks on a monthly basis in the own school, inviting all staff to participate. The process was introduced at a staff meeting by the team of teachers and administrators – and nearly half the staff voluntarily participated in the first month alone. By the end of the year 80% of the staff had been on at least one Walk-Through.

Each Walk-Through used the same focus question: "*What evidence do we see of students engaged in their own learning*," chosen deliberately for training and trust building. This allowed participants to ease into the process, while gathering lots of 'positive' evidence of the good things that were going on in their school. Debriefings were open to all staff, with the results shared through posters and electronic media.

In June of 2006, the entire staff gathered for a year-end celebration and reflection on their Walk-Through experience. Several key decisions came out of this event, charting the course for the 2006-07 school year:

1. The Walk-Through process is very successful, and it is time to use this tool to explore instructional questions in greater depth.
2. New focus questions need to be chosen, and they will be developed by teachers.
3. Since adult collaboration is one of the five school goals, participation will be mandatory for all. Exceptions may be made for first or second year teachers.

One teacher summarized their progress by saying that "we were ready to move beyond that 'safe and happy place' to a much deeper look at our own instruction."

### The second six months

When school opened in the fall of 2006, staff were anxious to get started on the Walk-Through process once again. The first step was to choose new focus questions. This process was accomplished by the whole faculty, with the principal setting out only one guideline – the questions needed to connect to the comprehensive school goals.

Team leader Ellen Maldonado says, "We had to come to consensus on what was most important to us. It would have been easier to create the focus questions myself, but not nearly as valuable. This open process ensured that teachers are tied to what they want to improve."

Small teams were formed, and they created four focus questions to start the year. These questions align directly with the school goals shown in the left hand column below.

| FOCUS QUESTION | SCHOOL GOAL |
|---|---|
| 1. What evidence do we see that students are applying reading strategies across the curriculum? | 1. To improve student achievement in reading for specific subgroups identified as not meeting AYP. |
| 2. What evidence do we see that students are involved in a variety of opportunities to investigate, explain, and/or demonstrate their mathematical thinking? | 2. To improve student achievement in mathematics. |

| | |
|---|---|
| 3. What evidence do we see or hear that the science focus question is promoting inquiry and problem solving for students? | 3. To improve student achievement in science. |
| 4. What evidence of social skills (CARES) do we see in support of academic learning? | 4. To establish a process of teacher collaboration focused on increasing student learning and school climate. |

Walk-Throughs are scheduled twice each month. Teachers typically walk in groups of four and visit three classrooms – so there are many opportunities for everyone to participate. Although first and second year teachers are exempt from the requirement to participate, most have voluntarily joined.

Scheduling time has been a challenge, but with a little creativity and flexibility it has been managed. Groups of teachers walk for about 45 minutes during the day, and are given an additional 45 minutes in the afternoon (NOT after school) for debriefing. Classroom aides, 'special' teachers (art, music and physical education) and administrators (as well as substitutes) have been used to free up time during the day for walkers. Time spent for Walk-Throughs has not impinged on planning or meeting time – the faculty as a whole did not want to give up that time.

The faculty at Six to Six has also created a unique tool to help them implement changes based on what they learn from each walk. This simple tool helps participants focus on what student behaviors and activities most impressed them during their walk. It also helps them be explicit about the task they take away – an individual commitment to try something new in their classroom based on what they learned during their Walk-Through.

At the end of the debriefing, each participant completes this sheet, making a commitment to one thing he or she will do. These sheets are collected and made part of the 'debriefing record' – being shared along with the notes.

# Figure 4- 1.  Six to Six Summary and Reflection Form

CWT Action Steps

Instructional and professional learning action steps are implemented between classroom walk-throughs to ensure continued progress towards our comprehensive school plan and the improved performance of all students.

| What impressed you today? | What might you try? | What ONE will you try? |
|---|---|---|
| * | * | * |
| * | * | |
| * | | |
| * | | |

## An evolving culture

Walk-Throughs are still a relatively new endeavor at Six to Six, yet they have already made a measurable impact on the school culture. "We now feel like a true professional learning community," explained one teacher.

Teacher Eva Kibby states, "I have found the conversations about instruction to be much deeper. They are tremendous! We're talking about how you do 'it' but also *why* you do 'it'. We're talking to one another about how effective programs are for our kids. We never did that before."

DuFour and Eaker's[3] groundbreaking work on professional learning communities has widely been accepted as the best and most comprehensive work in this area. They define six characteristics of professional learning communities:

1. Shared mission, vision and values
2. Collective inquiry
3. Collaborative teams
4. Action orientation and experimentation
5. Continuous improvement
6. Results orientation

Walk-throughs were introduced at Six to Six *to* build professional learning communities. Evidence of DuFour's PLC characteristics can be found throughout the school – and not just during the formal

---

[3] DuFour, R. & Eaker, R. (1998) Professional learning communities at work: Best practices for enhancing student achievement. National Education Service: Bloomington, IL.

meeting times. Assistant principal Robyn Proto talks about how the nature of conversation at Six to Six has changed. She often hears 'little gems' – snippets of rich teacher conversation now heard in the hallways.

Many teachers received extensive training through the CSR grant, but even as the grant was drawing to a close they began to worry they would 'become islands again'. There was no mechanism for them to 'take from and build through' the different grades. They talked about feeling disconnected. Today the faculty describes the Walk-Through process as a way to deliver, evaluate and assess some of the ongoing professional development initiatives they have the opportunity to participate in. By identifying and examining important instructional questions with their colleagues, they have built an expectation of continuous improvement. The conversation is fed with evidence based on data and on observed student behaviors.

Teachers at Six to Six are spending more time looking at data, and using that data to drive the focus and inquiry of Walk-Throughs. In fact, the last round of state assessment scores (CMTs) were predicted by the teachers – they have a much better understanding of what skills students are mastering these days.

There used to be a 'monumental divide' between the elementary and middle grades at Six to Six. One school was CSR, one was not. One got lots of training, one got none. Resentments and misunderstandings abounded. The Walk-Through process has helped the faculty to unify and align different philosophical views. No one can say "It doesn't affect me" any longer. The process has helped to clarify the school vision, and more importantly, has given the teachers an authentic voice in determining where they are going, and how they are going to get there.

The Walk-Through process has taken a school with pockets of excellence to a results-oriented professional learning community, a place where people work together around a unified vision of where they are going and how they can get there together.

> *"The Walk-Throughs helped us create a climate where teachers feel safe and are encouraged to talk about their work. Now we feel we are doing the real work of school improvement."*— Classroom teacher, Six to Six Magnet School, Bridgeport, CT

# Chapter 5. Using Walk-Through Protocols to Improve Instruction

**Suva Elementary School, Montebello Unified School District, Montebello, CA**

> "It is like someone put on the lights. I see so much more. The climate is so energized as a result of the walks."—Program Director, Suva Elementary School

If you were to walk into the teachers' room at Suva Elementary School you would hear teachers sharing and exchanging strategies and ideas, and talking positively about their practice. The Walk-Through protocol has helped create an upbeat "can do" climate at the school. This positive climate has been reinforced by rising student achievement; in the six years since the school began using the Walk-Through protocol, the school has improved by 282 API[4] points.

---

[4] The Academic Performance Index (API) is the cornerstone of California's Public Schools Accountability Act of 1999 (PSAA). The purpose of the API is to measure the academic performance and growth of schools. It is a numeric index (or scale) that ranges from a low of 200 to a high of 1000. A school's score on the API is an indicator of a school's performance level. The statewide API performance target for all schools is 800. A school's growth is measured by how well it is moving toward or past that goal.

## The setting

Suva Elementary School, in the Montebello Unified School District, is a kindergarten through fourth grade school. It is located in the city of Montebello, California, an urban, lower economic, industrial community approximately five miles east of the Los Angeles Civic Center. Families are drawn to the community because of its proximity to jobs, and its many affordable multiple family dwellings. Population is dense, contributing to the urban feel of the community. Suva's 897 students attend school on a single-track, year-round schedule. Almost 97% of students receive free or reduced-price lunch, and 78% are identified as English Language Learners.

| Current school enrollments by gender/ethnicity | |
|---|---|
| American Indian/Alaskan | 0 |
| Asian/Pacific Islander | 1 |
| Black | 1 |
| Caucasian | 14 |
| Hispanic | 881 |
| TOTAL ENROLLMENT | 897 |

Suva Elementary
6740 East Suva St.
Montebello, CA 90201
Phone:      (562) 927-1827
Web Site    http://www.sue.montebello.k12.ca.us/

Beatriz Flores, Principal

### The Mission and Goals

*The mission of Suva Elementary School is to provide a supportive and nurturing educational environment in partnership with students, parents, and the community that enables every individual to reach his/her full potential by promoting positive self-esteem, a lifelong love of learning, and an appreciation of cultural diversity.*

Suva identified three specific focus areas for attaining these goals:

1. Creation of a professional learning community that promotes high expectations and fosters a climate of collaboration, collegiality, and communication;

2. Classroom use of research-supported practices in:
   - higher order thinking skills
   - the writing process (with fidelity and frequency)
   - problem solving and reasoning in mathematics
   - Specially designed academic instruction in English and interactive strategies for English Learners; and

3. Meaningful professional development that uses a variety of structures, settings, and practices.

## Getting Started

In 2000, Suva was among the lowest performing schools in the state. Its API (California's Academic Progress Index) score showed "growth" of minus 73 points; no subgroup reached its target.

There were many theories surfaced to explain Suva's poor academic performance:

- *Lack of a clearly articulated plan for reaching school goals.*

- *Sporadic and fragmented professional development.* Teachers had many opportunities to attend district and county conferences and workshops, but they had no process for sharing their new learning with the rest of the faculty. They said they would prefer to focus on learning a few strategies in depth, rather than attend disconnected one-time-only workshops.

- *Lack of follow-through and accountability.* Many new strategies and practices were introduced, but applied inconsistently due to lack of knowledge, communication, and accountability. Teachers felt frustrated with the lack of support, direction, and follow-through.

- *Lack of communication.* Teachers had few opportunities to talk to each other about their work. Grade level meetings did not use their time together for reflection and conversation about teacher practice or student work. While one grade level team did decide to meet on their own time to coordinate their planning and assessment, other grade levels did not.

Because of their poor showing on the API, Suva was designated as an II/USP (Immediate Intervention/Underperforming School Program) school by the State of California in 2000-2001. The school chose UCLA SMP as the state-mandated External Evaluators ("EE") to help them create a new plan of action, and to monitor its implementation.

The initial findings of the EE team indicated that Suva was a school poised for change, but lacked tools and structures to make that change happen. The teachers strongly believed that all students could achieve, and projected a willingness to move ahead to improve student achievement. They were unclear, however, about how to proceed.

The school's early objective was to create a professional learning community—reflecting their belief that this was a necessary condition for success. They wanted clear expectations, effective communication, and professional collaboration as the framework of their reform. After creating their action plan, Suva's leadership team (one representative from each grade level, one literacy coach, and one administrator) selected SMP's Walk-Through protocol as the process for this new collaborative way of working. In addition to providing the needed structure and focus, Walk-Throughs could also provide opportunities to identify ongoing professional development needs. The Walk-Through protocol would become the vehicle to address issues of looking at student work and teacher practice.

The leadership team was then trained in the Walk-Through process and began the process of collecting authentic data, learning about the current reality, and talking about their findings. Grade-level meetings were reorganized to focus on student work and teacher practice. Teachers started talking about what students were doing and why, and what new learning was needed.

## After the first year

During the first year, only the leadership team participated in the Walk-Throughs. It soon became evident that the true impact of this process would result only when everyone participated.

In the summer of 2001, ten additional faculty members attended the UCLA SMP Walk-Through Institute. From that point on, all faculty members walked the school every month in rotating teams, visiting every classroom. Administrators arranged for substitutes to ensure that every teacher had an opportunity to participate at least once during the year; many participated more than once.

Walk-Through teams consisted of teachers from each grade level, administrators, parents, and external consultants. Four teams of four to five people visited approximately ten classrooms each. Teams walked from 8:00 a.m. to 10:30 a.m. and debriefed the walk from 10:30 a.m. to noon. The debrief was video-taped and made available to grade-level meetings. Walk-Through teams charted their findings and hung the charts in the faculty room. Findings were also typed up and shared with the entire faculty at faculty meetings. Feedback from all who participated was positive.

Over time, the Walk-Through format changed, depending on the needs that were identified. Sometimes teams walked a "vertical" slice of K-4 classrooms. At other times teams walked through classrooms on a their own grade level or to classrooms one grade level above and one below their grade.

Action discussions took place at grade level meetings. Grade levels used the protocol to talk about the questions raised by the Walk-Through. Teachers listed options and needs and decided on an action step, such as a new classroom practice or a suggestion for additional professional development. Grade levels also developed the focus question for their next walk.

The administration was responsible for supporting the grade levels in implementing their next steps. The leadership team met with the principal every week to share grade level discussions and actions.

Walk-Throughs, paired with regular grade-level meetings focusing on student work, created a culture of improvement that raised the quality of instruction in all classrooms. Observers noted pockets of student growth, and adopted the specific literacy and English Language Development strategies that appeared to be most effective.

A specific change of practice resulting from a Walk-Through occurred in math. Assessment data indicated Suva students were performing poorly in demonstrating math problem-solving skills. As a result, teachers had all agreed to use a math problem-of-the-week, believing this targeted, regular practice would help their students refine their problem-solving skills. A Walk-Through and subsequent discussion revealed that some teachers used the problem as a learning experience, some as a formative assessment, others as a summative assessment. While everyone was doing it they were in fact employing different strategies in their classrooms. Through discussions tied to observable evidence of students working to solve problems, teachers learned from one another and adopted a consistent, effective practice that led to the student outcomes they desired. The results? Increased performance on benchmark and state assessments.

A distinguishing feature of the Suva Walk-Throughs was that all teachers participate in the walks and all classes are visited. In the beginning, the administration and the UCLA SMP team assumed the responsibility for organizing the Walk-Throughs. However, within six months the teachers themselves had taken on this role. The leadership team assumed responsibility for the organization, scheduling, and follow-through of the monthly walks. This team facilitated the process before the walk, developed the norms, led the debrief, and presented the results at staff meetings.

## Evidence of Improving Instruction

### API Evidence

API data reflect an overall increase of 282 points in five years, or an average of 56.4 points per year.

| Year | Score | Growth |
|------|-------|--------|
| 2000 | 356 | -73 |
| 2001 | 449 | +93 |
| 2002 | 496 | +47 |
| 2003 | 582 | +86 |
| 2004 | 610 | + 28 |
| 2005 | 638 | +28 |

Staff at Suva remark that it is the Walk-Through culture that has led to this dramatic growth in student achievement. Teachers are talking to each other differently. Grade-level meetings revolved around issues and questions that surfaced during the Walk-Throughs. Grade levels shared their experiences and implemented or refined new practices. Even skeptics quickly realized that the process really was non-judgmental and non-evaluative, and they too began to implement new practices. The Walk-Through protocol, now completely managed by the teachers, became a central part of the school culture.

For Suva teachers, the Walk-Through Protocol built a strong foundation for collaboration and collegiality. By creating a culture of open classrooms, it deprivatized practice. It gave teachers a protocol through which they could look at their own and others' work. It supported meaningful dialogue around topics that had previously been seen as threatening. It helped transform Suva from a top-down hierarchy to a very democratic school culture focused on student learning. As a result of this process, teachers are now looking at evidence to support implementing teaching strategies that lead to continuous improvement for both students and teachers.

"I have been walking through classrooms for three years and every time I learn something new, and I am re-enthused about learning and teaching."—3rd Grade teacher, Suva Elementary School

# Chapter 6. Using Walk-Through Protocols to Unify a District-Wide Culture of Student Achievement

**The Antelope Valley Union High School District**

> "Districts need simple, systematic processes to turn individual achievement into collective results. The Walk-Through protocol helps us see positive patterns and trends and build on them district-wide."—Assistant Superintendent, Antelope Valley Union High School District, Lancaster, CA

Now that educators in the Antelope Valley Union High School District participate in regular Walk-Throughs, a shift in professional conversation is occurring. Talk about strategies teachers use with students is augmented by talk about how students themselves understand and use the strategies to scaffold their own learning. A district-wide culture of common expectations is developed by learning together across all eight high schools.

### *The setting*

The Antelope Valley Union High School District, anchored by the peaks of the San Gabriel and Tehachapi Mountains and encompassing a broad swath of California's Mojave Desert, serves more than 25,000 students. Amid the austere beauty of the desert, the cities of Lancaster and Palmdale, each with more than 100,000 residents, unite with the region's smaller towns and unincorporated areas to send students from thirteen different elementary school districts to AVUHSD's eight comprehensive high schools, and three alternative campuses.

The population served by the District has grown tenfold over the last twenty-five years, and with rapid growth have come all the complexities of an urban school system. In just a generation, the Antelope Valley has changed from largely rural and white to richly diverse, with the parents of many students commuting to distant jobs in Los Angeles.

| Current school enrollments by gender/ethnicity | |
|---|---|
| American Indian/Alaskan | 153 |
| Asian/Pacific Islander | 970 |
| Black | 5,551 |
| Caucasian | 7,714 |
| Hispanic | 11,891 |
| Female | 12,920 |
| Male | 13,359 |
| TOTAL ENROLLMENT | 26,279 |

More than twenty percent of AVUHSD's students are English Learners. Thirty-nine percent meet criteria as socio-economically disadvantaged, and twelve percent qualify as students with disabilities.

All students must pass the California High School Exit Exam to graduate, and school and district efficacy is measured against the growth targets set within California's Academic Performance Index (API) and federal Average Yearly Progress (AYP) expectations.

Though only seventy miles northeast of the city of Los Angeles, desert and mountains combine to create an isolated educational community. District educators, under the direction of Superintendent David Vierra, have undertaken the challenge of improving results from within, relying on their in-house expertise to implement research-supported instructional strategies. The Walk-Through protocol has helped them build the professional learning community that leads to continuous improvement of instruction and resulting improved student achievement.

Antelope Valley Union High School District
44811 Sierra Highway,
Lancaster, California, 93534
Telephone 661.948.7655
Website http://www.avdistrict.org/

David Vierra, Ph.D., Superintendent
Michael Vierra, Ph.D., Assistant Superintendent of Educational Services

## The Mission and Goals

The Antelope Valley Union High School District's stated mission is *"to provide a safe and secure learning environment that promotes a rigorous curriculum and enables students to develop the necessary academic, technical, and work-related skills of the 21$^{st}$ century. Every student who graduates will be prepared to pursue college or any career to which he/she aspires."*

To take the mission from statement to reality, AVUHSD has established the priority areas of:

- Students and Staff
- Safe and Supportive Schools
- Communication
- Facilities

In creating the "Students and Staff" priority area, AVUHSD has recognized that settings—scheduled times, places, and processes for student and professional learning—are essential to student development of 21$^{st}$ century academic, technical, and work-related skills. Thus, over the last three years, the District has acted on the hypothesis that significantly-improved student achievement will result from research-supported teaching and learning strategies implemented within a data-driven cycle of improvement. Professional inquiry spotlights the essential link between instruction and student learning. Professional learning communities are the settings in which inquiry becomes professional learning and development.

## Using the Walk-Through protocol to enhance inquiry in a professional learning community

When David Vierra was named superintendent of the AVUHSD, the district chose a leader who was a life long resident of the Antelope Valley, he knows the District and Antelope Valley's people well. His recently completed Ph.D. studies linked his relationship with the community and his curiosity about how to help the district be the best it could be. Guided by his own research experience, he and other AVUSD leaders set about bringing the latest research about strategies that work in high schools to the whole AVUHSD community of learners.

The McREL (Mid-continent Research for Education and Learning) meta-analysis of instructional strategies associated with improved student learning was the district's starting point. The practical book, *Classroom Instruction that Works,* by Robert Marzano, Debra Pickering, and Jane Pollack[5] translated the meta-analysis into practitioner-friendly strategies. In 2004-05 the District purchased the book for all schools and began a comprehensive district administrator effort to learn from the book. They chose to focus on four of the ten strategies: Summarizing and Note Taking; Reinforcing Effort and Providing Recognition; Cues, Questions, and Advance Organizers; and Similarities and Differences.

In 2005-06, after a year of working together on implementing the strategies, AVUHSD approached the UCLA School Management Program to initiate a part-

---

[5] Marzano, R., Pickering, D. & Pollack, J. (2001) Classroom instruction that works: Research-based strategies for increasing student achievement. Association for Supervision and Curriculum Development: Alexandria, VA.

nership to deepen the work and enhance the student achievement effects of their existing Administrator Professional Learning Community's study. Soon, instructional coaches began learning together as their own PLC, too.

Administrators and coaches began to ask—*What differences in student learning are we seeing based on our work with these strategies?* That question sparked the district's interest in finding a process that would help them tease out the impact of their emphasis on strategies. The Walk-Through protocol was the approach that fit their inquiry model and allowed all professionals in the district, not just administrators, to participate and benefit from collecting observable data, and debriefing its effect in the setting of the professional learning community.

## Getting Started

Professionals in the Antelope Valley Union High School District didn't have the luxury of devoting four days away from the Valley to attend SMP's *Walk-Through Institute.* Yet, the need and the energy to get started was palpable. So, in the 2005-06 school year, administrators and instructional coaches set out to begin the process in a less formal way. They decided to use part of their dedicated PLC time to learn about Walk-Throughs in a *virtual* setting. The setting had to be virtual because concerns about safety and supervision precluded all administrators being away from school during school hours— administrator PLC meetings were scheduled from 3:30 to 7:30 PM.

Administrators kicked off their experience by watching a 30-minute video overview of the Walk-Through protocol. They used snippets from teaching strategy videotapes to practice "observing like a video camera," and collecting evidence without judgment. Finally, they framed focus questions appropriate to their own school's circumstances to guide their work. They then took their focus question and the observation graphic back to their own sites, committing to spend 5-7 minutes in at least three classrooms, observing and recording evidence, and to share their data with their colleagues.

At the next monthly PLC meeting, observation graphics were reviewed, and the debrief protocol was followed. They talked about the evidence in pairs and triads to surface observed trends and patterns, and then talked again to elicit the probing questions that would lead to next steps in their inquiry. All groups began with the focus question: *What evidence do we see of students engaged in their own learning?* Some schools found the discussions resulting from that focus question so valuable that they continued with it through several sessions. Other schools quickly personalized the question to reflect specific professional development experiences unique to their sites and the outcomes they wished to observe in student work. By the end of the series of administrator and coach PLC's, most school teams had found it helpful to use the focus question as a lens for exploring the impact of the research-supported instructional strategies outlined on the previous page. A typical focus question was phrased as: *What evidence do we see of students using cueing and questioning to scaffold their own learning?*

Walk-Throughs for instructional coaches were initiated in the same way, but because coach PLC time was scheduled at a school site during the regular school day, coaches were able practice Walk-Throughs during PLC meetings. Coaches used the trends and probing questions they identified in the debrief portion of the protocol to frame dialogue about their coaching practice.

Near the end of school year 2005-06, principals met to assess the value of the PLC emphasis on Walk-Throughs as an instructional improvement tool. The intention from the beginning was to have administrator and instructional coach Walk-Through experiences create the foundation for initiating school-level teacher Walk-Throughs. Teachers in grade levels and departments would frame the focus questions on which they most wanted data. They would feed the results of the debrief back into their own collaboration with colleagues to enhance practices in the classroom. Though a few schools had already included teachers, many administrators felt that they needed facilitated Walk-Throughs at their own sites to support the extension of the practice. It was agreed that Walk-Throughs would continue the next school year, that the Administrator PLC would be restructured so that administrators might also experience facilitated walks at each other's sites during the regular school day, and that formal support for initiating teacher Walk-Throughs in each school would be provided by UCLA SMP.

## Building capacity throughout the district

With the opening of school year 2006-07, Walk-Throughs became a universal process that opened school and classroom doors, and made non-judgmental observation of students at work a focus of professional dialogue and planning. Instructional coaches continued to hone their coaching skills by using the trends, patterns, and questions that grew out of their Walk-Throughs at different sites. Administrator meetings were restructured to allow Walk-Throughs during school time. One half of a school's administrative team participated in a school-site Walk-Through followed by role specific professional dialogue once a month on Tuesday. The other half of the team came to the same site on Wednesday. Principals were always present on Tuesdays, and assistant principals, who are site coordinators of curriculum and instruction in AVUHSD, were always present on Wednesdays. The rest of a school's administrative team was divided evenly between the days. The Administrator Professional Learning Community still met after school hours so that the whole administrative team could be present at the same time, and build on their discrete Walk-Through experiences.

At the visitation sites, teachers continued to volunteer to open their doors. Though the process remained voluntary, by mid-year most schools reported that teachers were so comfortable with Walk-Throughs that all were happy to be visited.

Perhaps some of the comfort with inviting "walkers" into classrooms grew out of the specific school-site support that was provided to individual schools. Principals had asked to have SMP bring its "virtual" CWT introduction to each school to make sure that there was common understanding of the process across the district. The request became a commitment to provide the initial introduction to the whole school, and then to follow-up with three Walk-Throughs on each campus. SMP faculty began by serving as facilitators, gradually made the transition to coaching each site's teachers toward facilitating the protocols themselves.

Because each school is different, Walk-Throughs are evolving differently at each site. Some schools have embraced the protocol as a school-wide tool. They schedule Walk-Throughs on a regular basis at calendared intervals, using the same focus question throughout the school.

Other schools have chosen to implement Walk-Throughs in conjunction with department or grade-level collaboration time. In these schools, departments often frame different focus questions that are specific to instruction and student learning in their content areas.

At one site, a school focus on enhancing student engagement led two teachers to wonder how students defined "engagement," and what kind of instruction students believed helped them to be "engaged." The teachers' PLC decided to query students. They created several randomly selected student focus groups and asked students:

- What does it look like when a student is engaged in challenging learning?
- What best helps you learn?
- What hinders your learning?

A student panel shared the charted records of the focus discussions with the whole faculty, and then posted them at the entrance to the school library for all to see and ponder. The student responses were enlightening, and bore out research on student engagement. Students wanted interactive lessons that relied on discussion and questioning more than lectures. They wanted to see students themselves demonstrating problems and concepts, and to have assignments that were tied to real life applications of the material they were studying. A significant learning for all—teachers and students—was that asking student opinion directly proved to be "engaging" in itself. The school has decided to expand the process, and in the future, students will have the opportunity to participate in the Walk-Through process with their teachers.

## *An evolving tool in an evolving culture*

Like many districts taking on the challenge of educating all students well, the Antelope Valley Union High School District has found that it takes more than choosing a tool and training district personnel to use it.

Even as Walk-Throughs became a regular part of the school and district culture, AVUHSD teachers and administrators saw a need to talk about who they were as a district; to know what they value; to discover how the processes they choose further what they value. A Professional Learning Community asks substantive questions about what it wants to accomplish, what to do to get there, and especially, how to do it systemically with integrity and alignment.

In the Antelope Valley Union High School District, a focused look at achievement of No Child Left Behind targets served as a call to action. Choosing which action to take was a question of values. The selection of the Walk-Through protocol rested on answers to questions like: How do we transform student achievement results while we continue our historic self-reliance? How do we improve results while we build on the small-town atmosphere that continues to attract new residents to the area? What are the values represented by the image of "small town?"

Only in retrospect is it possible to trace a journey. After three years, the educators of the AVUHSD are now asking:

- Are we framing questions in ways that honor the commitment, expertise and hard work of students, professionals, and community members?
- Is our use of data helping us see and act on patterns of possibility?
- What difference is it making in student learning and achievement?

In Chapter 4 we cited the characteristics of the Professional Learning Community identified by DuFour and Eaker:

1. Shared mission, vision and values
2. Collective inquiry
3. Collaborative teams
4. Action orientation and experimentation
5. Continuous improvement
6. Results orientation

The AVUHSD case study moved beyond the characteristics that need to be present for a group to call itself a PLC—the **what.** The Antelope Valley Union High School District sought to discover the beliefs and values its processes must encourage within the PLC—the **how.** The AVUHSD discovered that it wanted processes that:

- Surfaced information in ways useful to different professional roles within the district—processes that simultaneously supported district administrators, school site administrators, and classroom teachers as they thought about their own practice and made immediate application to their work;
- Created meaningful dialogue among professionals who were beginners and others who were more experienced—processes where each would learn from the other;
- Invited comfortable participation—processes that managed personal style so that conversation could be inclusive and equitable across differences; and,
- Appreciated what was already present in the work of the AVUHSD—processes that used a cycle of improvement to identify and build on strengths. The district sought to achieve its goals by enhancing its achievements, to help them realize their goals.

Professionals in the AVUHSD were able to simultaneously *learn* and *apply* the Walk-Through protocol as part of their Professional Learning Communities' cycle of improvement. Because educators changed practices and saw measurable changes in student learning, NCLB growth targets seem less daunting, and reaching targets is more personally satisfying.

"Since starting Classroom Walk-Throughs, our observations have become less superficial. They are targeted, informed by data, and they have a direct impact on classroom practice. We have discovered an effective way of moving beyond our first opinion."—Teacher and Instructional Coach, Antelope Valley Union High School District, Lancaster, CA

# Appendix A. Sample, Three-Day Training Agenda

*Agenda Day One*

8:30 am      **Coffee and conversation**

9:00      **Welcome, introductions and purpose**

Desired outcomes
* Understand that Walk-Throughs provide a professional development tool that supports improved classroom practice
* Know collaborative strategies that build trust and support authentic data collection without judgment
* Be prepared to act as a leader and example in promoting the Walk-Through process in their own schools

9:20      **Linking classroom visits to our lives**
*Accessing our prior experience*

10:00      **Nuts and Bolts of a Classroom Walk-Through**
*Reading: Chapter 2*

10:15      **Break**

10:30      **Developing a learning community through class-room walk-throughs**
*The Walk-Through video: Overview of the non-evaluative observation process*

11:30      **Logistics of school visits—getting organized to walk**

| | |
|---|---|
| 11:45 | **Lunch** |
| 12:30 | **A Video "Virtual" Walk-Through** <br> *Looking for observable data* |
| 1:30 | **Debrief of the virtual Walk-Through** |
| 2:45 | **Review of logistics and agenda for tomorrow.** <br> *Homework—Reading Finn article using the insert method* |
| 3:00 | **Debrief of afternoon and 3-minute essay** |
| 3:15 | **End of day one** |

*Agenda for Day Two*

9:00 am      **Site visits—participants meet at assigned school site for facilitated walk**

11:45      **Overview of day two—reconvening**

12:00      Lunch

12:45      **Observations, perceptions, and assumptions**

1:15      **Experiential Learning**
Concentric Circles

2:30      **Logistics check-in**
**Homework for tomorrow—reading on useful questions**

3:00      **Reflection and 3-minute essay**

3:15      **End of day two**

*Agenda for Day Three*

9:00 am          **Second site visit**

11:45            **Overview of day three—Reconvene**

11:50            **Organizing to impact complex issues and achieve results**
                 **Working lunch with your group**

1:15             **Coaching trios:  A protocol to fine-tune planning**

3:00             **Final reflections, next steps**

3:15             **Three-minute essay and adjourn**
                 End of the institute, but really just the beginning

# Appendix B. Developing Group Norms

**OBJECTIVES:**
As a result of this activity, participants will develop their group norms.

**ACTIVITY: (APPROXIMATELY 1 HOUR)**

**Step 1: Introduction (3 minutes)**

*What are norms? Why do we need them?*

Groups generate norms as a way of deciding how to work and/or learn best together. Norms are a kind of contract that is generated, owned, and enforced by the group. Norms can range from rules that support productivity and respect for everyone's time, such as "be on time," to norms that establish expectations for personal and professional growth, such as "encourage and welcome different perspectives."

**Step 2: Individual Brainstorm (5 minutes)**

*What do we need from one another in order to learn and be able to take the risks needed to do so?*

Participants will generate a list of whatever they feel they need. Then, each participant will review his/her list, and pick the top three non-negotiable needs.

**Step 3: Small Group Negotiation (7 minutes)**
In pairs or trios, participants will share their top three needs, and pick two or three needs that they all agree are non-negotiable.

**Step 4: Collection and Charting of Needs (15 minutes)**
Each group will share its non-negotiable needs with the whole group as directed by the facilitator. The facilitator will chart the needs generated by the group.

**Step 5: Review Charts to Clarify Meaning (20 – 30 minutes)**
Clarify the words on the charts. Be specific by asking:

*What would it look like if this were happening?*

The facilitator will consolidate the overlapping needs, make a new chart, and present it to the group for approval.

The norms belong to the group. The norms will serve the group to the extent that the group follows them. Each member of the group will be given permission to enforce the norms. They are THEIRS.

# Appendix C.   A Sample Activity for Determining Next Steps

Instructional and professional learning action steps are implemented between classroom Walk-Throughs to ensure continued progress toward the school's vision of high-level learning and achievement for *all* students.

As the last step of the debrief, determine your next steps. In some fashion, whether by using colored dots or check marks, members of the group may select three areas they want to know more about, or see more of.

Ideas for next steps may then be shared and charted. These may include faculty professional development, sharing of instructional strategies, collaborative planning, review of student work, etc. They may take place in a variety of settings—faculty meetings, grade level teams, committee meetings, and so on.

## NEXT STEPS

| We want to know more about … (or see more of …) | What do we need to know? | What possible actions could we take? | What is the ONE thing we will agree to do? |
|---|---|---|---|
| • | • | • | • |
| • | • | • | |
| • | • | • | |

# About the Authors

**Laureen Cervone** is the Associate Director of the Northeast Region of the UCLA School Management Program. She provides consultation and support for states, districts, and schools related to the role of leadership in improving schools, specializing in working with leaders in low-performing schools in both urban and rural areas. Prior to her tenure at UCLA, Cervone worked with The Education Alliance at Brown University in the area of Leadership for Low-Performing Schools. A resident of Rhode Island, she holds an M.A. from Rhode Island College and a B.S. from Cornell University.

**Patricia Martinez-Miller** is Director of Faculty of the UCLA School Management Program. She lives in southern California where she and her SMP colleagues work in schools and districts to improve student learning through enhanced leadership and structured professional inquiry. Prior to joining UCLA SMP in 1993, Martinez-Miller was a teacher and principal in the Los Angeles Unified School District, and served as a governing board member of the South Pasadena Unified School District. She holds B.A., M.A., and Ph.D. degrees from the University of Southern California.